THE
BONSAI
BOOK

THE BONSAI BOOK

by ROBERT W. KING

RUNNING PRESS

PHILADELPHIA · LONDON

9   8   7   6   5   4   3   2   1
Digit on the right indicates the number of this printing

Library of Congress Cataloging-in-Publication Number
2001087065

ISBN 0-7624-1042-6 (package)

Package and book cover design by Mary Ann Liquori
Interior design by Johanna S. Roebas
Edited by Susan K. Hom
Typography: Herculanum, and Hiroshige
Bonsai were created and photographed by Robert W. King

This kit may be ordered by mail from the publisher.
Please include $2.50 for postage and handling.
But try your bookstore first!

Running Press Book Publishers
125 South Twenty-second Street
Philadelphia, Pennsylvania 19103-4399

Visit us on the web!
www.runningpress.com

To Jack Billet, my teacher, mentor and friend;
the Brandywine Bonsai Buds, who makes bonsai
so much fun; and Emily, Rebecca and Jessica,
who show me the beauty in this world.

CONTENTS

vi

PREFACE

Although there are many books on the market that describe the basics of bonsai, I have tried to make this one distinct by not producing a step-by-step guide of how to take a raw piece of plant material and transform it into a bonsai ready for display. But instead I have attempted to create a handbook that provides a basic understanding of not only what bonsai artists do when creating bonsai but also why they do it. It is my hope that this information is not useful only to budding bonsai enthusiasts but also to a wider audience.

I would like to express my gratitude to the members

of the Brandywine Bonsai Society, the Delaware Valley Bonsai Study Group, the Brandywine Bonsai Buds, and the Monday Night Study Group for sharing their knowledge, enthusiasm, and love of bonsai so freely with me. I am indebted to my family for their understanding and support as I became more and more obsessed with both bonsai and this project.

Lastly, I would like to acknowledge Susan Hom for her understanding, encouragement, and editorial skills and Running Press for giving me this opportunity.

INTRODUCTION

In the West, the word bonsai has been shrouded in mystery, confusion, and misunderstanding. From the way it is pronounced, (bone-sigh, not bon-zeye which literally means, "10,000 years," and was used in World War II as a war cry by Japanese soldiers) to what it represents. Bonsai is the phonetic translation of two Japanese characters that literally means "plant" (sai) in a "shallow tray" (bon). However, bonsai represents much more than any plant in a shallow tray. It is a centuries-old art form in which the principles of artistic design and aesthetics are combined with sound and established horticultural practices to create an idealized, miniaturized recreation of nature.

It has long been thought that the art of bonsai was restricted to those experts who had a deep understanding of Asian culture and a spiritual commitment to creating bonsai. In fact, the ability to create a bonsai is within the reach of anyone. However, like most art forms, the more time and effort one puts into the study of bonsai, the more accomplished the artist will become. Bonsai artists range from those that have one or two very small bonsai on the balcony of their apartment in the city to those who have dedicated gardens containing hundreds of trees ranging in size from six inches to six feet.

To begin to create bonsai, all you really need is a tree or shrub from a garden center, a pair of gardening shears and scissors, some bonsai wire, and a good set of instructions. With a little bit of effort and dedication, you can be off on a wonderful, lifelong creative journey that can fill your life with beauty, serenity, and peace.

HISTORY OF BONSAI

In the West, most people associate the art form of bonsai with Japan. However, bonsai actually has its roots in China. Approximately two thousand years ago, the Chinese literati, men of great wealth and education, would travel from the cities into the countryside to contemplate nature, write poetry, and paint. They soon discovered that they could also create artistic representations of nature by collecting small trees from the countryside, placing them in pots, and training them to resemble their full-size brethren. Using techniques still practiced today, these early bonsai artists created trees

1

that had the look of majestic, old trees that had weathered the extremes of nature and survived.

Buddhist monks and merchants traveling between Japan and China introduced the art of bonsai to Japan around the twelfth century A.D. In Japan, the art of bonsai evolved to its present-day form as the Japanese artists simplified the traditional Chinese style. The number of trees in the pot was reduced to a single tree; rocks, figurines, and other plant material were removed from the design; and the pot became an integral part of the composition. Japanese bonsai became more graceful in feeling and form than the Chinese style. Moreover, the movement that was introduced into the trunk and branches by the artists flowed much more smoothly and natural than the dramatic and extreme angles found with Chinese bonsai.

The introduction of bonsai to the Western world began during the Meiji Dynasty when Japan began exhibiting example of masterpiece bonsai at World Fairs in both the United States and Europe. However, it wasn't until the end of World War II, when American servicemen returned from the Pacific Theatre with stories of the magnificent little trees that they saw in Japan, that bonsai took a foothold in North America. Bonsai really did not become an art form widely practiced by Westerners until two bonsai masters of Japanese ethnicity independently decided to share their bonsai knowledge with people from the West. Yuji Yoshimura and John Naka, each on a different coast of the United States (Yoshimura was on the East Coast and Naka on the

West Coast) began to organize classes and study pro-
grams for Westerners with an interest in bonsai.

In 1957, Yoshimura published his book, *The Japan-*

Japanese white pine (Pinus parviflora)
Informal upright style

ese Art of Miniature Trees and Landscapes: Their Cre-
ation, Care, and Enjoyment. This book was the first in
English to describe the art of bonsai in such a way that
was understandable to Westerners. Gone were the refer-
ences to such bonsai styles as "Flying Dragon" and

"Springing Tiger" and in their place, Yoshimura categorized bonsai into five basic styles: formal upright, informal upright, slant, semi-cascade and full-cascade. It

Chrysanthemum
Informal upright style

was Yoshimura's simplification of bonsai design and techniques that allowed thousands of people to first try their hand at this Asian art form.

John Naka's two-volume set of books, *Bonsai Techniques Volume I and II* (published 1973 and 1982 respectively), elaborated upon as well as added to the information presented by Yoshimura. The information in Naka's books was not presented as a step-by-step guide on how to create a bonsai from start to finish but was organized more in an encyclopedic fashion meant to be studied and reviewed over and over. Still today, Naka's two books are considered the "bible" of published English-language bonsai information.

Today bonsai continues to gain popularity outside of Japan. If you are interested in pursuing your interest in bonsai beyond this kit, there are a variety of available resources such as clubs, conventions, symposia, videos, magazines, and public gardens, which are devoted to the creation, care, and display of bonsai.

General Bonsai Characteristics

APPROPRIATE PLANT MATERIAL

Almost any woody plant material is appropriate for bonsai. Its botanical classification can be as tree, shrub, or vine specimens. However, there are certain characteristics that contribute to the aesthetics and perceived age of the tree that you should look for when selecting bonsai material. One of the parameters that separate the masterpiece from the average bonsai is scale. The trunk, branches, twigs, leaves, flowers, and fruit should all be in scale with one another. A small bonsai with leaves that are one-tenth the size of the tree looks unbalanced and contrived. Likewise, a medium-sized apple tree

Japanese red maple (Acer palmatum 'kiyohime')
Twin trunk style (In training)

bonsai with several large apples on it not only looks out of scale but also threatens the well-being of the tree.

When looking for appropriate plant material, you should look for plant material that naturally has small leaves. A good rule of thumb to use when evaluating leaf size is that once the tree is confined to a pot, the size of the leaf will reduce by approximately 50 percent.

Chinese elm (Ulmus parvifolia)
Informal upright style

Likewise, plant material that has compound leaves (leaves that are composed of a central stem with several attached leaflets) does not reduce well and rarely looks in scale. For example, Japanese and trident maples and

Chinese elms have leaves that are naturally small, readily reduce in size, and have the added benefit of having spectacular displays of autumn color. Evergreen trees like Japanese garden juniper, and mugo and scots pines have small needles that will reduce even more upon confinement of the tree to a pot.

While it is possible to reduce the size of the leaf, it is impossible to reduce the size of the fruit or flowers. Therefore, it is imperative that one looks for species of trees in which the fruit and flowers are of small size. There are bonsai artists who love to experience the changing seasons with their trees, so they specialize in flowering and fruiting bonsai. Instead of creating a bonsai out of domestic apple where the fruit will never be in scale of the tree, you can use a variety of crab apple that has extremely small fruit. Another good species of fruiting tree to use as a bonsai is cotoneaster. This tree has naturally small leaves, takes well to life in a container, and has very small fruit that is in scale with a bonsai. However, if you come across an example of a tree that would make the perfect bonsai except that it has large fruit, don't pass it by. Instead, by thinning the number of fruit on the tree during the fruiting period to just a couple of perfect fruit, you can overcome the problem of scale.

As with fruit, it is not possible to reduce the size of the flower either. The suggestions above for fruiting bonsai also apply to flowering bonsai. One should select species and varieties of plants that have naturally small flowers.

One of the most common flowering plants used for bonsai is the azalea. Azaleas have flowers that can range in size from three-eighths to three inches in diameter. By staying with the smaller-flowered varieties, it is quite easy to create flowering bonsai in which the flowers are in scale with the rest of the tree. Again, if the perfect material presents itself, but the flowers are too big to be in scale with the rest of the tree, by limiting the number of flowers to just a few, you still can have a fantastic bonsai.

Along with flower size, you have to be concerned with flower color. Most novice bonsai enthusiasts believe that a good bonsai should shout out, "Look at me!," to the viewer and one way to accomplish this is to use flowering bonsai that have bright, vibrant, almost neon colors. However, just the opposite is true. A good bonsai should shout out, "Look at me!," not by being the flashiest but by being designed, maintained, and displayed so perfectly that the viewer gets a feeling of harmony and serenity from looking at the tree. Ideally, a photograph of a tree that excluded the pot should look like a tree in nature. Thus, it is much better to use varieties of trees that have softer colors. For example, soft pink instead of fuchsia, creamy yellow instead of hot yellow, and light purple instead of neon blue.

Another trait that you should look for is good ramification, which is the division of branches into secondary and tertiary branches. The greater the ramification, the greater the impression of age. Trees like azalea, Japanese and trident maples, Chinese elms, and zelkovas can easily create highly ramified bonsai. Finally, rough bark is highly desirable in a bonsai since a tree with naturally rough bark presents an image of great age. Pines,

Japanese zelkova (Zelkova serrata)
Broom style

junipers, crab apples, and Chinese elms all will develop attractive rough bark with time.

Plant material that have been found to be excellent for bonsai:

Conifers—Japanese black, white and red pines, Jack pine, mugo pine, scots pine, Chinese junipers, Japanese garden and needle junipers, hinoki cypress, and yew

Deciduous—Chinese and Japanese elms, Japanese and trident maples, Japanese and European beech, and hornbeams

Deciduous Conifers—Japanese, Chinese and American larch, dawn redwood, bald cypress, and gingko

Fruiting—Crab apple, cotoneaster, Japanese and Chinese quince, mulberry, porcelain-berry, and pear

Flowering—Azalea, rose, wisteria, forsythia, honeysuckle, bitter-sweet, and serissa

BONSAI SIZES

Most people not familiar with bonsai believe that these tiny trees are genetically stunted to be small. In reality, bonsai trees that are removed from the pot, planted into the ground and allowed to grow unhindered will attain their normal height. It is through continuous branch and root pruning that the bonsai stays small.

Bonsai can range in size from a tiny tree only a couple of inches high in a pot not bigger than an inch wide to one that is five feet tall in a pot that takes four people to carry. Likewise, forest plantings can be created that are made up of the minimum number of trees and can fit in the palm of the artist's hand to ones that may contain more than one hundred trees and need a pot six feet in length. Most bonsai artists will gravitate towards trees of a certain size. However, trees at either extreme have certain requirements that should be considered.

Very small bonsai have the advantage of not taking up much room, so a person with a limited space for growing bonsai can have a larger number of trees in their collection. In addition, the pots and the raw plant material for small bonsai are usually cheaper than their bigger cousins, allowing a person with a limited budget to build up a collection of smaller trees and still stay within a certain limit. However, smaller trees have a smaller soil volume and may require watering and fertilizing more often. Also, it takes considerably more artistic skill to design small bonsai since they usually only have a very small number of branches and leaves and any mistakes in the design are painfully obvious to the viewer.

The other extreme is the extremely large bonsai. These are usually in excess of three feet and have the ability to stop a viewer dead in their tracks at a bonsai show. The obvious disadvantages to bonsai this large are the space required to grow and keep these trees as well as the additional help required just to move them. Other disadvantages are the extreme costs of the pots, soil, wire and tree material necessary for extra large bonsai and the amount of time necessary for pruning, wiring, and pinching to keep the bonsai in good shape. The advantages to bonsai of this size are that with the large soil volume in the pot, these trees require less watering and fertilizing, are easier to protect from freezing in winter, and are at less risk of being stolen. In addition, since these trees have more branches and foliage than their smaller siblings, small errors in design or care are easier to hide.

Most bonsai collections of novice enthusiasts contain trees somewhere in between these two extremes. As the artists mature and gain experience as bonsai artists, they will begin to feel confident enough to begin to experiment with trees of these extreme sizes.

BONSAI STYLES

In 1957, Yoshimura in his book, *The Japanese Art of Miniature Trees and Landscapes: Their Creation, Care, and Enjoyment*, categorized bonsai into five styles based on the line of the trunk. These styles are formal upright, informal upright, slant, semi-cascade and full-cascade. There are now additional styles but these are not based on the line of the trunk but are based on environmental representation or the number of trunks in the design and will be considered later.

A trunk that has no curves and is perpendicular to the soil surface characterizes the formal upright style. This style represents a tree that is growing in a mild climate unhindered in an open field or meadow. The lack of competition with other trees for sunlight and the mild climate allows the tree to grow straight and tall.

Japanese black pine (Pinus thunbergii)
Informal upright style

Although the bonsai created in this style will usually lack the movement and the regions of deadwood that are common in bonsai designed in the other styles, it still should include elements that invoke the feeling of great age. These include a wide expanse of surface

15

Japanese black pine (Pinus thunbergii)
Slant style

roots, a thick trunk, branches showing the effects of gravity by approaching the horizontal. In addition, the movement of the branches should be consistent with the trunk and be designed without curves.

The informal upright style is very similar to the formal upright in that the apex of the tree should be in line with the bottom of the tree. (See photograph on page

16

15.) However, between the apex and the bottom, the trunk will contain several curves. This style represents a tree that is in an environment in which it has had to battle wind, rain, snow, ice, and be in competition with other trees for sunlight. The curves in the trunk were formed by directional adjustments the tree made during its life in order to improve its chances of survival. Since the branches undergo the same stresses as the trunk, the branches of informal upright style should also con-

Satsuki azalea (Rhododendron indicum)
Semi-cascade style (In training)

tain movement. For consistency, the severity of the curves in the trunk should be similar to the severity of the curves in the branches.

Like with the formal and informal upright styles, the apex, the tree being higher than the bottom of the tree characterizes the slant style. (See photograph on page 16.) The main difference between slant style and the other two upright styles is that the apex of the tree is no longer directly over the bottom of the tree. Instead, the apex of the tree is positioned to the left or right and

Satsuki azalea (Rhododendron indicum)
Triple trunk

slightly to the front of the bottom of the tree. This type of tree mimics a tree that is in a vigorous competition with other trees for sunlight, pushed by continuous wind or weighted down by winter after winter of snow and ice.

The other two styles, semi-cascade and full-cascade, are characterized by having what is normally considered the top of the tree lower than the bottom. The difference between these two styles is the relationship of the top of the tree with the pot. In the full cascade, the top of the tree is below the bottom of the pot, whereas in the semi-cascade, the top of the tree falls somewhere between the bottom of the trunk and the bottom of the pot. (See photograph on page 17.) These styles represent trees that are growing off the side of a cliff or canyon and are pulled down by gravity and/or the weight of ice and snow.

The other styles used to categorize bonsai are not based on the line of the trunk but instead the number of trunks in the design or the representation of a certain environmental situation. Multiple trunk styles include twin trunk, triple trunk, grove (five or seven trunks), and forest (greater than nine trunks). In all these multiple trunk styles, one tree is dominant and the other trees are submissive to the main or "number one" tree. (See photograph of triple trunk style on page 18.)

There are several styles that represent certain environmental localities. Single trunk styles include root-over-rock, exposed root, driftwood, and literati styles. The multiple trunk styles include raft and clump styles. The root-over-rock style mimics a tree in nature whose roots have grown in a thin layer of soil that was later removed by erosion to expose the roots and the rocky underlayer. The exposed root style imitates the tree that

Juniper (Juniperus sp.)
Driftwood style

is growing on a river bank whose roots have slowly been exposed to air by the annual erosion of the river bank by flooding and melted snow. The driftwood style represents the trees that grow along the sea shore and mountain tops that have large areas of exposed deadwood due to the constant "sandblasting" from salt water, beach sand, and ice crystals. The deadwood on bonsai designed in this style usually is found naturally on collected trees or created by the artist with woodworking equipment.

The multiple trunk styles—clump, sprout, and raft—represent trees that for some environmental reason have had to make severe alterations in their growth pat-

Crape myrtle (Lagerstroemia indica)

Sprout style

tern. The clump style represents a group of trees that are growing in very close proximity. Over time the roots of the trees have intertwined and fused together such that it appears to the casual viewer that there are several trunks originating from one root mass. The sprout style is very similar to the clump style except that the multiple trunks all originate from one tree. In this case, it represents the situation in which the parental tree has been broken off close to the ground and several new buds have taken over as new trunks. The raft style mimics the tree that has fallen over but survived. The area of the tree that comes in contact with the earth forms roots, whereas those branches not damaged in the fall start to grow towards sunlight and take on the characteristics of trunks.

The literati (also known as bunjin) style can be used with single or multiple trunk bonsai and is closer to art from the minimalist school than the representational. Although sometimes described as a tree that has spent its life battling the best that nature could throw at it and still survives, it is better described as an abstract representation of the spirit of this epic battle. The term literati comes from the fact that these trees resemble the calligraphy paintings of the literati, Chinese men of great education and wealth that retired from the cities to the country and spent their days in the contemplation of nature and transferring their thoughts and philosophies into sculpture, painting, and poetry.

The literati bonsai usually has a long, thin trunk that

contains a great amount of graceful and dramatic move-ment. It has only the minimal number of branches necessary for the health of the tree and these tend to be located at the top. Also, it is common for the literati bonsai to be designed such that a significant amount of deadwood is visible. The long, thin trunk can be thought to represent the long but precipitous life the tree has experienced. The graceful but dramatic movement of the trunk and branches represents the graceful but

Japanese black pine (Pinus thunbergii)
Literati style

23

dramatic dance the tree has had to perform in order to survive, while the deadwood and the limited number of branches show the permanent scars that the tree has

Hinoki cypress (Chamaecyparis obtusa)
Literati style

obtained from its lifelong battle.

All the styles described above that are not based on the line of the trunk are usually paired with one of the styles that are. For example, a forest planting can be designed in the formal or informal upright styles; a literati bonsai may be in the slant style; or a root-over-rock bonsai may be in the semi-cascade style. Usually the categories based on the trunk line dictates the movement of the tree and the one not based on trunk line dictates the environmental feeling.

Selection of Bonsai Material

There are several ways in which you can acquire plant material for bonsai. These range from buying a bonsai that has been designed and trained by another artist to starting plant material from seed. Each method has its own advantages and disadvantages depending on the time and commitment you want to dedicate to bonsai.

The easiest method for obtaining a bonsai is to purchase one that is well along the development pathway. These can be found at specialty bonsai nurseries, garden centers, and gift shops at public gardens and arboretums. The differences between the trees available

26

at a specialty nursery versus the garden center/gift shop are quite distinctive. The first thing you will notice is the discrepancy in price. The trees available at a specialty nursery are usually quite a bit more expensive. This is because these trees are often either collected from the wild or imported from Asia, whereas those available in the garden centers are usually mass-produced from one- or two-year-old cuttings. In addition, at the bonsai nursery, the trees have been further developed and cared for by a bona fide bonsai artist or their apprentice, while at a garden center, the only follow-up care they receive is a daily watering.

Local bonsai clubs are another source for bonsai trees. Most clubs have small sales tables at their meetings and an annual sale/auction in which members are able to sell their extra trees. The owners of these bonsai usually have already started styling the tree and are willing to part with the tree at a reasonable price. One will have the advantage of meeting the seller of the tree who can provide instructions on the care of that particular tree and can always act as a resource in the future. Moreover, by getting involved in the local bonsai club, the new bonsai enthusiast will have opportunities to add to their bonsai knowledge, meet and take classes from visiting artists and interact with a group of people who all share an interest in bonsai.

Another method for obtaining suitable material for bonsai is to collect from nature. This may involve trips to the mountains to digging up and keeping old shrubs from a neighbor's landscaping project. The greatest advantage to this method is that, with some diligence, you may be able to find aged material that has had a lot of design work already done by nature. The disadvantage to this method is that it may require much time and exploring to locate suitable material. Moreover, when the perfect material is found, it may be on private property where you are required to get permission from the owner or even worse, it may be on government property where the removal of plant material is illegal.

Once a tree is located and permission is granted for digging, the difficult task of removing the tree comes next. This may take several return trips to the collecting area to root and branch prune the tree until there is no risk that the tree will die once it is removed from the earth and placed into a container. However, it is becoming easier to obtain collected material without actually digging it yourself as bonsai nurseries and vendor areas at bonsai conventions and symposia are now starting to carry a good selection of collected material of all sizes and price ranges.

The best location to obtain quality plant material at a reasonable price is at one's local garden center. If you are not afraid of getting down on your hands and knees and getting your hands dirty, there are bonsai treasures to be had in the long rows of trees, shrubs, and vines found in the landscape section. At the nursery, these trees will look nothing like a bonsai but with a little creativity and imagination you should be able to see the hidden bonsai in the untrained tree. Look for a thick trunk with a nice flair at the soil line and a gentle taper from bottom to top, a good selection of branches, and foliage close to the trunk. Most of all, you want the tree to be healthy and free of pests and disease. These plants can be taken home and styled into a bonsai or saved for a club workshop with a visiting bonsai artist.

The final way to obtain bonsai material is by propagation by seeds and cuttings. This is by far the cheapest method but also the one that will require the most time between beginning the project and having a bonsai. Seeds and cuttings are readily available and usually are free for the asking but you need a certain amount of horticultural skill and patience to create a tree ready for bonsai development from a seed or cutting.

Horticultural Requirements

Like all plants, bonsai need sunlight, water, oxygen, and nutrients for survival. In most cases, supplying these to the bonsai tree is no different than caring for a houseplant or outdoor-container planting. However, each species of tree has its own requirements for these elements and the successful bonsai artist must become educated in the needs of each of the species with which they are working. For example, a pine bonsai requires full sunlight during its growing season and cold temperatures during its dormant period. An azalea bonsai needs to be sited in dappled sunlight to shade during the growing season and cold temperatures during its dormant period. A fig tree bonsai needs full sunlight during the summer but must be protected when temperatures get below 60°F.

For a tree to be healthy and vigorous, which is one of the main goals of creating beautiful bonsai, it must be supplied with sufficient sunlight. The best way to accomplish this is to grow the tree, no matter the species, outside from mid-spring to mid-autumn. This guarantees that the tree will receive not only ample sunlight but also the proper amount of air circulation. Good air circulation is critical to the health of the bonsai. The movement of fresh air around the tree will assist in keeping it disease- and pest-free, as well as keeping the leaves free of dust. Another method for keeping the tree clean and pest- and disease-free is to thoroughly wash the foliage every time the tree is watered. If the bonsai is in the house for any period of time, the foliage should be regularly washed to keep it clean. This can be accomplished by filling a mister bottle with water and a couple drops of liquid dishwashing soap, placing the tree in the sink or bathtub, and thoroughly spraying the leaves.

Watering and fertilizing of the bonsai need to be performed on a regular basis. The rule of thumb for watering is to water whenever the soil is dry. For most bonsai, this translates to watering every day during the summer and every day to every second day in spring and fall. During winter, the trees, if placed indoors, should be watered every other day. If winterized in cold storage, the trees need to be watered about every seven to ten days.

There are many different types of fertilizers on the market, some marketed especially for bonsai. Until the bonsai enthusiast becomes extremely familiar with the needs of the trees, the best type of fertilizer to use is a balanced formulation that is marketed for houseplants. Bonsai need to be fertilized approximately every two weeks using the fertilizer at one half the recommended strength as stated on the fertilizer's label. During the winter months, those trees that were brought indoors should be fertilized once a month with quarter-strength fertilizer, while those outside under winter protection should not be fertilized at all.

ARTISTIC CONSIDERATIONS

A bonsai is more than a tree planted haphazardly into a pot. It is an artistic representation in which the artist uses well-established artistic principles to create his or her idea of a large, old tree that has survived the extremes of nature (e.g. snow, ice, wind, heat, drought, and disease) and has lived to tell about it. This can be accomplished by taking the characteristics that make up an old, rugged tree and incorporating them into the design of the bonsai. The best way for the artist to accomplish this is to let nature provide the inspiration for the bonsai design and combine this with well-established aesthetic elements.

VISUAL ELEMENTS

There are four visual elements—line, form, texture, and color—that must be considered when undertaking any artistic endeavor. When used correctly by the artist, these four elements will allow him or her to create an artistic piece that exhibits harmony and balance, and invokes an emotional response in the viewer.

Line: The line of an object is the way that the eye moves when viewing the piece. In bonsai, the movement of the trunk best expresses the line. It is the line of the bonsai that dictates in which style the tree will be designed. Since it is this line that directs the movement of the eye when viewing the bonsai and the artist wants the viewer's eye to move smoothly from the bottom of the tree towards the top without any interruptions, it is imperative that the tree gently tapers from the bottom to the top of the tree. This tapering of the trunk acts as a directional key so the eye knows which way to move. Another directional key is the distance between successive branches. The branches at the bottom of the trunk should have the greatest separation between them and the distance between branches should decrease as you move up the trunk.

If the trunk has movement (i.e. curves) in it, it is important that the severity of the curves is consistent along the entire length of the trunk. This consistency allows the eye to move steadily and smoothly toward the top of the tree. Drastic changes in the curves cause the eye to pause along the way and to back up to compare the curvature. Moreover, this consistency in the curvature of the trunk should be extended to the branches. For example, a straight trunk should have straight branches, whereas a curved trunk should have curved branches.

Japanese garden juniper (Juniperus procumbens 'nana')
Informal upright style

Form: The form is defined as how the space around the line is utilized. In bonsai, it is how the branches, deadwood, and foliage are used to create the outline of the tree. This not only is critical for the beauty of the tree but can help the artist suggest the age and locality of the tree. There are two types of space that the artist must make good use of for the tree to be truly spectacular. These are referred to as the positive and negative spaces. The positive space is the area that is filled by the

Maidenhair tree (Gingko biloba)
Twin trunk, flame style

trunk, branches, foliage, and deadwood. The negative space is the empty spaces in the foliage mass of the tree. It is essential for the bonsai artist to remember that both are equally important and must be given much thought when designing the bonsai.

The general form of all bonsai is the triangle. This is because this shape gives the bonsai visual stability without being static. However, one of the most common mistakes that the novice bonsai artist makes is to design all his bonsai in the shape of the Christmas tree. While this is appropriate for formal upright pines, dawn redwoods, bald cypress, and cedars, it is unnatural for most deciduous trees, azaleas, and junipers. These trees should be styled with a rounder apex and a softer outline. The best way to determine what the outline of a bonsai should be is to observe the outline of the same species of tree in nature and mimic it.

When creating the form of the bonsai, the artist uses the scalene triangle as a model. The scalene triangle— one in which the three sides are of three different lengths—demonstrates strength and stability while giving the impression of movement to the eye. The overall triangle form, made by drawing imaginary lines from the apex of the tree to the corners of the pot, can be made into a scalene triangle by potting the tree just to the left or the right of the centerline of the pot. A smaller scalene triangle should be formed with the foliage of the tree. This can be accomplished by having the first and second branches (counting from the bottom up) of the tree at different levels. The third scalene triangle that should

37

be used in the design of the bonsai is the one that is formed from the foliage pads of each individual branch. The area of the foliage pad closest to the trunk should be widest from side to side and thickest from top to bottom. The foliage pad should thin out and narrow as it moves away from the trunk.

The use of negative space in the design is important in that it allows the viewer to see the movement of the individual branches and the definition of the foliage pads. Moreover, it gives the viewer rest stops to pause before moving onto the next part of the tree. A saying in bonsai design pertaining to negative space is "A bird in scale with the tree should be able to fly unhindered between successive branches." If this guideline is followed, the proportion of positive to negative space should be fine.

Color: Color affects the beauty of an object by giving it a sense of unity and emotion. Colors that harmonize well together will allow the line and the form to stand out to the viewer. It should assist the artist in invoking the intended emotional response. A color scheme that does not harmonize well will lead to confusion and visual awkwardness. This confusion prevents the viewer from experiencing an emotional response to the piece. In bonsai, color has many different roles in the design of the tree. The most obvious one is the color of the foliage. Although the artist wants to present an image of great age, he also wants the tree to appear healthy. Therefore, a good deep, rich color of foliage is highly desirable. However, the foliage does not always need to be "grass" green. The artist should feel free to use foliage that contains hints of reds, blues, and purples but should stay away from those tints in the yellow and gray range as they give the impression of poor or declining health.

The color will also influence the viewer's sense of the season. The bright green flush of buds on the branches of the larch and the flowering of the wisteria, crab apples, and quince herald the glory of spring. The deep, rich colors of foliage on the deciduous trees, the flowering of cotoneaster and satsuki azalea, and the fruiting of the crab apples all mark summer. The bright oranges and crimsons of the maples and the yellows of the gingko will let the viewer know that they are looking at an autumn display. It is the lack of color that best exemplifies winter. The browns and grays of the trunks and branches of the deciduous trees and the muted greens of the junipers and cedars all set the tone of a winter display. However, a winter display does not necessarily have to be colorless, the pink and white flowers of the winter-blooming flowering apricot always act as a ray of hope for spring in the winter display.

Color, also, plays a critical role in tying the whole composition together. It is critical that the color of the foliage, flowers, fruit, bark, and pot all harmonize well. Many people incorrectly think of the pot as just a container to hold the bonsai soil or as being similar to the frame around a picture. In bonsai, the pot is an essential part of the composition. A pot of the wrong color has the ability to destroy the beauty and feeling of a wonderful tree.

Almost any bonsai can be placed in an unglazed earthtone pot, especially those that are brown, gray or terra cotta. Moreover, evergreen conifers should always be placed into an unglazed pot of a color that harmonizes with the foliage and bark of the tree. Glazed pots are almost exclusively used with deciduous trees, especially those that fruit and flower. When matching the color of the pot with the tree, the artist first has to decide what is the most important aspect of the tree. Once this is decided, he or she can decide what color pot to use. For example, a pot can be chosen such that its color complements a tree's autumn color, the color of the bark in winter, flower color during spring, or the color of the fruit during summer.

Pot colors usually contrast with the selected highlighted element of the trees both in shade (light versus dark) and color (warm versus cool). Well-chosen contrasting shades of color will accentuate the tree's best features. For example, a dark blue pot will set off the pale pink flowers of an azalea, a light blue pot will accentuate the dark red fruit of a crab apple and a light cream pot will highlight the deep green foliage of a hornbeam. The other type of contrast that the bonsai artist must consider is color. This involves using warm and cool colors together to highlight the tree. For example, red and yellow are considered warm colors, whereas blue, and green are considered cool. Usual warm-cool combinations are red and orange with blue and green with yellow. Examples of this would be a flowering forsythia (yellow flowers) in a green pot, a pink flowered azalea or the orange fall display of a maple in a blue pot.

Texture: The last visual element that has to be considered by the bonsai artist is texture. Texture is found in the bark of the tree and the surface of the pot. Unlike color, where the bonsai artist strives for contrast of color and shade, the texture of the tree and pot should be consistent. For example, a rough bark tree like a pine is best placed in a pot that has a rough and grainy surface, whereas a smooth bark tree like a European beech is best in a smooth glazed or unglazed pot. Other parts of the pot that influences the texture are the legs, if any, the thickness of the walls, a lip on the rim of the pot, and panels or decorations on the sides of the pot.

BONSAI DESIGN PRINCIPLES

As important as line, form, color, and texture are to the aesthetics of bonsai design, they can only influence the beauty of the bonsai so much. It is when the principles of proportion, unity, balance, and symmetry are incorporated into the design that the bonsai truly stands out.

Proportion: The principle of proportion plays several roles in the creation of bonsai. It determines the height of the tree, the size of the pot, and the best species to use. It is the width of the tree at the soil line (nebari) that determines the height of the tree. A study of the famous Japanese masterpieces suggests using a diameter-to-height ratio of 1:6 to 1:10 (i.e. a tree with a 1-inch base should be six to ten inches tall). Interestingly, archeologists have determined that this is the same ratio of width to height that was used by the builders of Greek and Roman columns. Once this ratio is exceeded, the tree takes on the appearance of a young tree. Reducing this ratio results in a loss of taper and creates a tree that looks stubby and contrived instead of graceful and natural.

The height and width of the tree dictates the size of the pot to be used for displaying the bonsai. The width of the pot should equal approximately two-thirds to three-fourths the height of the tree. Likewise, the depth of the pot should roughly be equal to the width of the tree at the soil line. However, it is not unusual for the pots of fruiting trees to be twice the width of the tree's nebari. This is necessary to make sure the tree has sufficient water for the fruit. In addition, some species of trees, azalea for example, cannot withstand excess heat and require a deeper pot to keep the roots cool in the heat of summer.

As mentioned previously, for the bonsai to look natural, it is important that the branches, foliage, fruit, and flowers are all in proportion with the size of the tree. It is important to remember that bonsai should be designed to look like a tree. By careful selection of the trees used in the creation of bonsai, one should be able to create bonsai in which all parts of the tree are in proportion with the final size.

Unity: Unity is the concept that repetition and continuity is pleasing to the eye. A good example of this is demonstrated in the design of gardens in which the repetition of colors and plants are used to create a pleasing continuity throughout the garden. In the art of bonsai, unity is suggested by the repetition of movement in the trunk and branches. For example, if the trunk is straight from the soil to the apex of the tree, then the branches should also be straight. If the trunk is curved, then the branches should contain curves. Moreover, the sharper the curves in the trunk, the sharper the curves in the branches.

There should be continuity in the branches as your eye moves from the bottom of the tree to the top. The branches should all have the same basic movement. The largest and thickest branches should be at the bottom and the branches should become smaller and thinner as they progress towards the apex. Finally, the distance between the branches should become shorter as they approach the top of the tree.

The principle of unity also plays a role in the selection of the pot. Not only does the artist have to consider the relationship between the pot and tree with regards to color and texture but also shape. There should be consistency in the shape of the pot and the overall shape of the tree. A tree that has a softer, rounder outline should be placed in a pot that has a similar feel. For example, an oval or rectangular pot with rounded corners may be appropriate. Likewise, a tree with harsh angles in the trunk and branches and a sharp overall outline maybe more appropriate in a rectangular pot with sharp corners.

Balance: A common misconception is that a beautiful bonsai is one that is wildly designed with a twisting, grotesque trunk and branches coming out at all angles. However, the true masterpiece is one that exhibits great balance both in its movement and in its relationship with the pot. If we take the basic three-dimensional geometric shapes—the cube, sphere, and pyramid—we see that all three, in their own way, present a feeling of balance. The cube and pyramid give the greatest feeling of stability. Since in designing bonsai we want to present feelings of not only balance and stability but one of movement, the pyramid is the model we use when designing our trees. This also coincides with the Zen philosophy of the universe, in which the universe is pictured as a triangle, the two-dimensional form of the pyramid. The highest point represents Heaven, the lowest point, Earth, and the one in between, Man.

The most important type of balance to strive for is visual balance. No matter the style of the tree, it should look balanced and stable in the pot. For the formal and informal upright styles, this is easily accomplished. Using an oval or rectangular pot with the proper proportions will allow the tree to look balanced in the pot.

A tree styled in the slant or windswept styles is much more difficult to visually balance in the pot. There are three basic methods for creating a slant style tree that

American larch (Larix laricina)
Twin trunk, windswept style

is balanced in its pot. If the pot is round or square in shape, it should be extra deep and constructed to look heavy (e.g. dark, gritty clay, large feet, large outward-turned lip). This type of pot will give visual mass to the bottom of the design and will help to anchor the tree's visual mass. If the tree will be potted in an oval or rectangular pot, the pot may need to have extra width, up to one times the height of the tree, and the tree should be potted so that there is excess negative space on the side of the tree with the slant. In this way, the length of the pot on the side of the slant looks to support the tree. The third method for balancing the visual mass of a slant-style bonsai is to style the tree so the lower branches on the side away from the slant are exaggerated in length.

San Jose juniper (Juniperus chinesis 'San Jose')
Slant style

These branches will appear to act as a counterweight to prevent the slanting tree from toppling over.

With the semi and full-cascade styles, it is important

Ponderosa pine (Pinus ponderosa)
Informal upright style

that the artist matches the visual mass of the tree with that of the pot's, to create a bonsai that appears well balanced. Since trees that are designed into these two styles are almost always placed in round or square pots, the only way the artist has to adjust the visual mass of the pot is with the depth of the pot. Since the visual mass of the semi-cascade is adjacent to the pot and not over it as it is in the upright styles, the pot should be of approximately equivalent visual mass as the tree. If the pot is too shallow, the design will look unbalanced and the tree will appear as if it is going to fall over. If the pot is too deep, the tree will look small and out-of-place, and the design will lose its visual effect.

Like with the pot of the semi-cascade tree, the pot of the full-cascade tree is used to balance the design. Because of the length and shape of the cascading tree, it is more difficult to find the center of its visual mass. However, you must do this to select the proper pot. To select the visual mass of the cascade, you should draw an imaginary triangle that encompasses the outline of the tree. This triangle will roughly represent the visual mass of the tree. If you draw a horizontal line from the center of that triangle, that line should intersect the pot roughly in the middle of its depth if the pot is of the right visual mass.

Symmetry: When the bonsai artist applies the principle of symmetry to the design of a tree, it is actually asymmetry and not symmetry that he or she is striving for, as asymmetry gives the feeling of movement which is so important to the bonsai design. Previously, we discussed the geometric shape, the triangle for the model for bonsai design. However, it is the scalene triangle (one in which all three sides are of different length) that we use and not the equilateral triangle (one in which all three sides are of the same length). Both triangles give a feeling of strength and stability but only the scalene triangle includes the feeling of movement.

The bonsai design should include several triangular shapes. First, the overall visual mass and outline of the design should be in the shape of a scalene triangle. The overall outline of foliage of the tree when looking at it from the front and the side should be triangular. Each foliage pad on the branches should be pyramidal in shape with each side of the pyramid represented by a scalene triangle.

Even though a bonsai is usually viewed from the front, the artist must remember that the bonsai really has six sides: front, back, left, right, top, and bottom. The design principles—proportion, balance, unity and symmetry—must be applied to the design of the whole tree and should be evident when viewing it from any of the sides.

DISPLAY

DISPLAY IN A TOKONOMA

Traditional houses in Japan usually have a room for special occasions and overnight guests. Within this room is an alcove, known as a tokonoma, in which the family displays artwork, antiques, and family treasures. A bonsai is often the featured piece in the tokonoma.

Tradition dictates both the construction of the tokonoma and the display that is set up inside of it. The tokonoma is usually placed on the opposite wall of the doorway so people entering the room immediately notice it. It is also placed on either the right or left edge of the wall so that the exterior wall of the tokonoma can contain an outside circular window that allows natural light into the display. The floor of the tokonoma is slightly raised in comparison to the floor of the room. This protects the items contained within the tokonoma as well as gives them a superior siting. The tokonoma has two side walls. One, as mentioned above, is usually an exterior wall with a circular window in it and the other acts to frame the display and to visually block out the rest of the room. The ceiling of the tokonoma is lower than the ceiling of the room and, like the second wall, serves to frame the display contained within.

The tokonoma display should contain no more than three items which, when displayed together, suggest a locale and/or environment (i.e. mountains, seaside, meadow, etc.) and the season (i.e. spring, summer, autumn, or winter). Moreover, the seasonal suggestion of the display should agree with the season of the locale. For instance, during the winter, the tokonoma display should suggest winter.

When the tokonoma contains a bonsai, the bonsai should be the dominant item. The other two items should be a scroll and an accessory item, which may be a second, smaller bonsai, a small plant, a figurine, or an antique. The bonsai should be placed in the tokonoma on the side opposite the circular window. However, it is imperative, since plants are phototropic (they grow towards light), that the movement of the bonsai should be towards the window.

The scroll, which is hung in the middle of the back wall, should be simple and not dominate over the bonsai. Its main purpose is to help suggest the environment and season of the display. For example, in a winter display, a scroll with a watercolor painting of Mt. Fuji would be appropriate. In summer, a scroll with an ink or charcoal painting of bamboo would be suggestive of the rustling of the cool summer grass. In the case where the other objects in the tokonoma strongly suggest the season, the scroll may contain a poem written in calligraphy. However, the topic of the poem should be consistent with the season of the display. For example, if the tokonoma contains an ikebana display of spring wild flowers, the poem should be about springtime and not another season.

The third item in the tokonoma is an accessory item that helps complete the display. This item may be a small planting, figurine, antique, or if a bonsai is the main item, it may be a second, smaller bonsai. As with the scroll, the accessory item should be consistent with the artist's intent for the locale and the season. If the display in the tokonoma is created during the autumn and it contains a Japanese maple forest bonsai to show off the brilliant autumn colors and a scroll containing a watercolor painting of distant mountains and a flock of migratory birds, then the accessory item may be a small, antique bronze duck figurine placed on a legless, irregular-shaped stand made from high polished dark wood to represent a lake.

Placement of this accessory item should be on the

Tokonoma display with bald cypress

opposite side of the scroll than the bonsai (or main item), and closest to the circular window. It should be placed so that visual mass of the bonsai, the main subject of the scroll, and the accessory item forms a scalene triangle. In arranging the items in the tokonoma, one should be careful to place the main item equidistant from the front and back of the tokonoma and the accessory piece slightly forward or backward of the main item. How it is placed in relationship with the main piece depends on what keeps everything in scale.

DISPLAY IN A WESTERN HOME

Most homes in the West do not have special alcoves or areas for displaying art. Therefore, different guidelines exist for displaying bonsai in a Western home. It must be remembered that, for most bonsai, displays inside of a house are temporary. In a house with central air and heat, the humidity is lower than in the Sahara Desert. It is detrimental to a tree that is used to the outdoor conditions to be placed too long in such an arid environment. Therefore, a bonsai should not be displayed indoors for more than two or three days. Moreover, during the winter, a bonsai that is in dormancy should not be on display indoors for more than six to eight hours. Not only is the low humidity detrimental to the tree but the shift from a low temperature to a higher one may cause the tree to break out of dormancy. If this happens, the tree will require special handling for the rest of the winter.

When a bonsai is displayed in the Western home, it is usually displayed on its own without additional items. Since the bonsai will often be the lone item on display, it is important that it is shown properly. The bonsai should be placed on a display stand, which should be elegant but not dominate over the bonsai. Since a bonsai is a representation of nature, the stand itself should be made of a naturally occurring material. Most are made from wood or dried bamboo. The width of the stand should be approximately one and a half to one and three-quarters the width of the bonsai. The bonsai itself should be not placed in the exact center of the stand but instead should be placed farther from the side of the stand in which the movement of the tree is going. This increased negative space on the side of the movement of the tree increases the feeling of motion to the viewer.

The bonsai display should be placed in front of a plain background. This is easily accomplished by displaying it on a table against a wall painted a neutral color (whites and off-whites are best). However, if this is not possible, the bonsai can be displayed in front of screen that serves as the background. Screens that nicely serve this purpose are bamboo fencing, gold or silver-foiled screens, and Japanese shoji screens (paper screens that are mounted onto a wooden frame). Also attractive are the antique wooden boxes that were used to hold typesetting letters. These are usually hinged in the middle and can be set opened on its side to form a background. Highly decorated or inlaid screens should be avoided as these are too elaborate and will detract from the bonsai.

If an accessory piece is to be displayed with the bonsai, it should be appropriate for the tree and in scale. Commonly used accessory pieces for indoor displays are the Chinese mudmen or bronze animal figurines. If these are to be used, they should not be placed in the pot with the tree but should be displayed alongside on their own stand. If plant material is used for an accessory piece, it is important that it is in the proper scale. For example, if a grass planting is to be used as an accessory piece, the grass should not be longer than

Tokonoma display with serrisa foetida

one or two times the height of the tree's surface roots. Since most inside bonsai displays use trees of medium size, finding grass this short is near impossible. Therefore, to accomplish the same feeling, a small pot of moss can be used to represent the grass surrounding a tree in a field.

OUTSIDE DISPLAY

There are three ways to display bonsai outside depending on the purpose of the display. During the training phase, most bonsai are placed on growing or training benches. If the artist has many bonsai that are ready for display, he or she may have an area with show benches, or an outside tokonoma that is used to display exceptionally prized bonsai.

Training Bench Displays: The training or growing bench serves a more utilitarian purpose than an artistic one. It is used not so much for displaying bonsai but for keeping the bonsai safe and easily accessible while they are being trained. For most artists, the objectives behind the construction of the growing bench is not to create a display area that is visually pleasing to the eye but to make a sturdy bench that can hold the bonsai collection safely.

As stated above, the purpose of this area is to keep the bonsai accessible to the artist and to protect the bonsai from harm. There should be enough bench space so that the trees are not overcrowded. The trees should be placed so that they get sufficient sunlight, air circulation, and water. Also, they should be placed so that the artist can easily work on the trees since there is plenty of wiring, pruning, pinching, and weeding to be done during the growing season. Usually this can be accomplished by placing the bench surface at approximately waist height. The bench should be sturdy and able to withstand summer storms, wind, curious animals, and the wayward soccer ball.

A simple construction that is sturdy, easily adjusted, moveable, and temporary (can be broken down in the winter and reconstructed in the spring) is one made out of cinder or cement blocks and pressure-treated two-by eight-foot planks. The blocks can be stacked to the proper height and the planks placed across the blocks two or three planks wide. The weight of the bonsai will keep the planks from shifting so there is no need for additional fasteners or supports. This type of bench can be rearranged in the fall to construct a winter-storage cold frame for the bonsai which then can be made back into a bench in the spring. The ground underneath the bench should be level and covered with three to five inches of wood chips or small pebbles. This will prevent grass and weeds from growing underneath the benches, which will reduce the risk of damage to the bonsai by lawn-care equipment and will hold moisture that will increase the humidity around the trees and prevent the soil from drying out between waterings.

The Show Bench: If the artist has several bonsai that are ready for show, he or she may construct several show benches for display between public exhibitions.

Show bench display with chrysanthemum bonsai (planted on rock style)

Unlike the training benches, the show benches are usually constructed more artistically. The benches are usually set higher than the training benches so that the trees can be viewed at eye level without having to stoop

59

or squat down. The benches usually are of a more permanent construction and are made from higher quality
wood. The ground below the benches is covered with
several inches of wood chips or small pebbles, is kept
groomed and weed-free and may be decorated with
additional items to help set the mood of the display.
These items may include water basins, Japanese
lanterns, statuary, garden hose baskets, container
plantings of grasses or bamboo, and wind chimes. There
are usually benches placed strategically around the

Show bench display

display area so guests can relax in the garden and enjoy the bonsai.

The trees on the display bench are usually spaced farther apart that those on the growing bench. This is done to allow the viewer to look at one tree at a time without being distracted by adjacent trees. In addition, the trees may have accessory plantings accompanying them on the bench. Because of the risk of inclement weather, the trees and accessory planting usually are not placed on separate display stands. The exception may be when guests have been invited over to view the bonsai. The owner may place the trees on stands for the period that the guests are viewing the bonsai and then remove the stands once they have left. The trees themselves, when on the show bench, are usually kept impeccably manicured. New growth is regularly removed to keep the outline in shape, the soil in the pot is kept weed-free, and the pot is kept free of stains and water marks.

If space allows, the growing benches and display benches should be physically removed from each other. If they cannot be placed in different parts of the artist's property, a visual barrier of some type (e.g. bamboo fence, shrubs, outbuilding, etc.) should be placed between the two.

Display in an Exhibit

Most bonsai clubs host one or two shows annually in which their members can exhibit trees for public viewing. These exhibits are usually held in shopping mall public areas, museum lobbies, arboretums, public gardens, and nature centers, and may be accompanied by demonstrations in the art of bonsai.

Usually these venues provide tables for the club to use for displays and the club supplies the backdrops, table covers, etc. Backdrops and table covers should be simple and neutral in color so not to distract from the bonsai. In fact, a white backdrop with a tan, beige, gray, or green table cover is the perfect setting for a public display. When setting up a large display, it is important

Show bench display

not only to consider each individual tree and accessory piece, but also the relationship of the trees with those adjacent to them. The display should be set up so there are no two trees of the same species next to each other.

In addition, adjacent trees should vary in size and height but be consistent in terms of their movement. If several tables are going to be used, the movement of the trees can be used to direct traffic flow through the display and to certain areas of the display (for instance, the information table or demonstration area that the club wants emphasized).

As for the individual trees, they should be healthy, pest and disease-free, and in good color. The final pruning should have been completed several weeks in advance of the show so, there are no fresh wounds on the tree. Wiring should be absent from the tree. If some wire must be left on, it should be restricted to the present year's growth. Any dead or dying foliage should be removed. The trunk of the tree should be cleaned of all moss, mildew, and algae. Any deadwood on the tree should be cleaned with a brush and a diluted soap-and-water solution and then treated with a lime sulfur solution to prevent decay and to make the deadwood a uniform color.

The soil in the pot should be refilled if necessary to about one fourth of an inch from the top of the pot. Any weeds and solid organic fertilizer cakes, if used, should be removed. If it is part of the design, moss should be placed on the soil surface about a week before to the show to allow time for the moss to settle in and look more natural. The pot should be cleaned to remove all stains and water spots. The night before the show, unglazed pots can be lightly coated with mineral, baby, or butcher-block oil to enhance their appearance. A glazed pot should be polished with a soft cloth and then can be rubbed with a cloth that has been moistened with baby or butcher-block oil.

The trees and any accessory pieces should be placed on appropriate stands. Stands should be cleaned and polished. I have found that Murphy Oil Soap, used properly, cleans the stand and restores some of the wood's natural luster. The stand should be dried with a

Show bench display

soft cloth and then lightly coated with butcher-block oil. This will enhance the beauty of the stand as well as protect it from water stains.

As stated previously, the trees are placed on the stand so there is more negative space on the stand in the direction of the movement of the tree. It is important that the bottom of the pot be free of grit or anything abrasive that might scratch the surface of the stand. Likewise, if the bonsai show will take place over several days and the trees will need to be watered, they should be removed from their stands, watered, and not returned to the stands until the water has stopped draining and the bottom of the pots wiped dry with a cloth. Some artists will place a thin Plexiglas sheet on the top of the stand to prevent scratches and water spots. However, this detracts from the natural feeling of the display and distracts the viewer's eye.

CONCLUSION

Bonsai is a living art form that incorporates the design principles of aesthetics and the scientific principles of horticulture. Bonsai, being quite new to the Western world, is still very much rooted in Asian tradition. However, aesthetics, science, and traditions are forever evolving. As these continue to evolve and bonsai becomes more commonplace in the West, this art form should experience changes that make bonsai less of an "Asian" art form into one that is just another type of artistic endeavor. These changes will occur as trees and shrubs indigenous to the Rocky Mountains and forests of North America, the Alps of Europe, and the jungles of South America are used as raw materials; as Western potters start creating bonsai pots using their local clays; and as non-Japanese bonsai artists get together and experiment with new styles and designs based on the trees they see around them.

These changes are already starting to happen. Non-Japanese students are serving as apprentices to Japanese masters and are bringing back their newly acquired knowledge to the West. They are coming home and applying the Japanese traditions and their Western artistic philosophies to the trees they are finding in their locale to create new and exciting bonsai. Although these bonsai look very different than those found in our local garden centers, they not only should be admired but also should serve as examples of what we, as amateur bonsai artists, should strive for.

Most excitingly, what currently is taking place is a realization that we, as people from the West, no longer have to be intimidated by the pursuit of the art of bonsai. We now believe it is not necessary to be steeped in the Asian culture and tradition to create beautiful bonsai. Instead, we are realizing that, with a good understanding of aesthetics and what it takes to keep a plant alive, we are very capable of creating a work of art that we enjoy having around and are proud to display for our family and friends.

So please go out, get some trees, and start experimenting, but most of all enjoy yourself.